I hope this book
is of some inspiration,
Hope you enjoy,

The Paper Sail

Words of Faith and Inspiration

Trevor T. McCauley

CROSSBOOKS
PUBLISHING

CrossBooks™
A Division of LifeWay
1663 Liberty Drive
Bloomington, IN 47403
www.crossbooks.com
Phone: 1-866-879-0502

©*2010 Trevor T. McCauley. All rights reserved.*

No part of this book may be reproduced, stored in a retrieval system, or transmitted by any means without the written permission of the author.

First published by CrossBooks 4/8/2010

ISBN: 978-1-6150-7182-1 (sc)
ISBN: 978-1-6150-7183-8 (hc)

Printed in the United States of America
Bloomington, Indiana

This book is printed on acid-free paper.

The Paper Sail

Here I am patching together a paper sail
Attached to a dream and its bottomless lunch pail
Hoping to harness enough wind
Praying that the waves won't make me start over again

I put this together with paste, paper and glue
Words at their worth will stick when the sun beats through
Where is the witness that chides me to work?
Or the assurance this vessel needs more than to lurch

So I listen, I build, trying to seize whose will?
There creates the better of patience until
The Lord exacts upon what He means
This page gets ripped out, alas, I feel a breeze

The Beautiful Promise

These are the days of the unseen
And the anchored trust in the truth of His being
You cannot break ground, running
As you cannot suppose clarity without breathing into eternity
There is no waiting for the impossible to fall from the sky
So mount up on wings and catch it
That is your calling

You'll never be happy swimming in circles
That doubt and its submission hold
You were born a conqueror
You were made to transcend the loaded rules of this life
Yes to fly, yes, not just to break through the barriers
But to soar, to see, so that more can follow,
And more will live without fear as their reason to act
And fewer still will be stuck on the wrong side of the mountain
Let us be everything that His glory showed us
Let us be rich and rejoice in all that He has promised

Thanks

Tend to me Lord
And make my soul willing
For across the divide I loose the understanding
That this world knows
You have made me complete
There's nothing I can grieve for
That You've left apart
Something so wise and so still
Caresses me and knows there's more to fulfill
When I look and fathom
Once in perfect time always so righteous
Everyday that's what I find in You alone
Master Jesus
Thanks

The Life

Conceived,
Drawn from an outline
A periphery
Lines dancing light
An emulsion of possibility
There birthed is life
When you asked for direction
Pleaded before language
You asserted yourself
Innate became the definition
Bathed in time
Only now you don't need to be reminded
Echoes believed
Into maturity
And you understood
Cries in turn
Become answers
Patience behaved
Becomes a benefactor
The simple gift of life

Newborn

Open Book
A cradle with blue bars
I don't know how it is that I see you today
Rasping in voice, strung from little sleep
Moving in sheets, ah, yes you are home
Migratory and ambulatory
Little hands, little fingers rise and they fall
Your feet dance then they rest
In you is a promise hardly spoken
But weighted on my heart
Now freed in awe and wonder
From here the room is bright enough
To play, and highlights in your mother's hair
Smiles sink deeper
As I catch her eyes, honest
How everything in trust keeps a promise

Recycled Energy

Gifted strings of immortal happiness
Torn out of the drought of everything I missed
Sent from the edges of consciousness
Apparently stirred into the path of a swift
I remember the visions of a latter day
Consoled in the outcome, the greater gain
For it is your heart I am after,
Your grace covers all that matters
When I feel swallowed up in this world
And my purpose feels separate and blurred
Help me to find what I should put my energy toward
So I can deliver what is ultimately Yours

Walking With the Master

From where You enter in
I've been waiting
Listening for the root and the cause
Believing, no the truth isn't lost

All of this life is beginning
Just barely beginning
And it's been hard
But I will walk with You today
Oh, cause I know it is time
And You will change me
So enter in rearrange me
Until all the work is done

How I have shouldered everything
And gripped the reigns too tight
But I won't forget the yoke
No you're my master
Letting me be defined in this new peace
By design and by desire
Until You alone will uphold every talent
So goes the gifts You birthed
Oh, a long time ago

Totally

Draw me to You
Bear my true word
Keep sending me
Reaching for me
I don't live in the apology
I live in the promise

And when need becomes more than a posture
Desire feeds the complete evidence
That you are not wanting me
Wanting apart from wanton need
Capture me, all fulfilling

But I am already Yours
Just beckon me totally
Instill that there is no other want
That brings me to the spot
Where the lot that is my portion
Cannot be shaken
Never mistaken
Oh, I'm delivered and totally Yours

Eternity

Why do I look around
And think this is the eternity you gave me?
Because none of this is real
Everything I see and hear
That floods in
It doesn't shake me
Masquerading/tempting
Struggles attempt to hold their face value
Surface tension draws out unanswered questions
Yes I am still dreaming
And none of this is real

For I am only undivided
When it's not my language I hear
And it's the only sound
That takes my spirit straight to You
How much longer in the shadows of the real thing?
How much further, can we contain ourselves,
Making noise, fulfilling art for ourselves?
I just want to be home,
Where You make perfect sense
And all is championed and fulfilled
Be it in Your perfect love
Lord, let it rest

The Seeding of Vision

Space has known no distance
And time hath no divide
You have given me eternity
But I need You right now

From here visions birth new dreams
And are seen in full color
Their world is its prize to behold
And it reaches to the place
From where they've been placed in a mold
Poured out the design has its function

But what do I hold onto in this season?
What I have known as truth
To let go of these visions
Enough for them to become the seeds
I've left to die
Knowing through time they'll live and rise

Awaken me and be the difference
May the wisdom I know
Bring forth the patience that grows
Still breaking from the old shell
Beginning and seeking beyond the old self

From the fruit of a servant
Extends the root that takes hold
Below the surface
Knowing everything great
Holds a purpose
Defining its way

The Missionary's Song

As the heat trespasses upon dusty ground
Is it safe to pray aloud?
Has the wind brought confusion to our minds?
Can we offer up thanks even though we are blind?

This is the exhaustion that comes with everyday
Too long I have been removed by the wait
Silence eats up all the words we could exchange
For You know why, Lord, I am held at bay

But I am not alone
Buried in the distance
Here is but a wilderness
And this work of my heart is my witness

Here is the place called home
The only dream I've ever known
Some tease, saying it's far from heaven
Oh, but this is the life He owns

Check Your Bags

I don't know what yesterday was supposed to prove
It's an island bearing forgiveness
And whatever there was looking back
Be at the disarray, let there be poignant clarity:

Today remains far from those followers of whispers fate
As peace dreamt past the clues,
Becoming as well the evidence:
A kin-sister to truth

Looking sideways is not enough
We no longer stick to the ground
Lagging below/behind what we surmised as the past
For you are not a memory
Any more than I am a product of time

Take this instant
Let its master redefine what is settled now
No more going on with the fight
It will never leave here,
Tethered to your pride and insolence

For nothing I knew is going though the baggage claim
Tagged or otherwise
I am turning over,
I am waking within
Without cause's comparison

Now, forever settled--take it no further
There's the rescue and an answer
However decidedly small
Presence holds an offer to deliver you all

I Am Yours

The dream cascades down a mountain stream
And I'm listening to more that You give
Every intention fulfilled
Every thought
Know that in this light
I am Yours

This is the intricacy
This is the moment nothing can take away
Every need had a master
Every want a provider
But in this time
I'll give You the space
Undivided, I am Yours

Swimming into the next flow
My eyes dancing to and fro
Tantalized an unbroken code
It's just Your nature
Your being that holds me and doesn't let go
Teach me, You'll never leave me
This is Your freedom
This is Your light
Dancing around you captivate my senses
You are perfect without mention
I am Yours

Oh Perfect Desire

Every definition ran off the page
Simply daring me to return to the evidence
How it is that You made me
Oh, I have a lot to learn
For You are cordial, You listen
And time is just a defense-ordered-pasture
Where piled high are not laments
To wait is only to squeeze another wrinkle
My eyes still pleading to contain their sorrow,
Yearning for something beyond their recognition of sight
No, the choice is to mine
But You chose me
You make me yearn for You
I am Your child
Of eyes that are set upon this sure posture
That is the aim, to seek You Lord
Oh perfect desire

Hope

Oh, the breeze leads me to the shore
Far from yesterday's before
So I'll hoist the sail-raise the anchor
Knowing today I must live for,
You and You alone

There's a peace that understands
It flows through me on this path
Prayers carry over-urge me to steer
Into deeper waters akin, to all that I fear

All aboard in the hope of Your salvation
You provide the Way and the light in my direction

Where is my home?
Well, you're rocking the boat
Where is your home?
Well it's far away

But there is my hope
In prayers I never spoke
But there is my hope
It's what I needed most
It's what You've given me!

As sure as the shoreline clings back to the sea
Waves on the beach roll incessantly

The Remnant

We are the consecrated, the concentrated
And we will stay here
Look at what they've left
Empty houses, abandoned dreams
Scattered lives
How are we the chosen?
For I have seen the weary fall and go elsewhere
But somehow this remnant never took the sane way out
Faced with the tough choices to remain
Steadfast, secure in the one who provides
We're poised to hold on
For we declare it is a new day
And we will see this city rise

A Voice Turned Over

Am I the one who's standing here?
My voice has gone somewhere else
I cannot command
Somehow I'm turning over
Breech control
Oh, tell me this is the real me
And this is everything

What is it that suffers,
Upon the weight of what I call myself?
Some feet tall
First name and all
Whispers can knock you down
Appointed words can release the prisoners

How are we really captive?
From a voice rains down heaven
A spirit true in dedication
There's a heart bent on heading home
It knows something
It knows something

September 12, 2001

I don't know how to begin again from here
All this subsistence of time is belittled with time
I don't know what has survived to move on
This "better" trial exists under the heir of responsibility
We are now taken up with the thieves that won't give back time
For what we've seen, there are too many shadows
To know the depth of the hour
How must our lives change, we are ever in a moment, of air unprepared?
So who keeps watch, those of which in urgency never needed to
We are now in a trance, the subject of a potent act
What can now springs us awake, did someone let another in
To prey upon the towers, fields and government walls?
While shaking inevitability through our minds
If somehow we knew better, why didn't we?
All battered waves know where to recede
How many scary dreams are sprung forward
Into the manifestations of a different need

Ignition

I'm not waiting for the same sense to follow me
Let it be the pure thought
Pouring out the changed light

In this vision seeded so
Rising to top a difference
Reflections of the truest self, not the same landscape,
Scenes repeated as a sitcom lost in syndication
Affirmed only in afterthoughts and adjusted punctuation
Breath taking, visibly threatened
A season literal read straight through the soul

Ignition why do you burn, efficient
Pick me up, adjust, call me forth
From the reason, show me more

The Moment

There is abundance in the moment
Truth in Your dear word
What is left unsatisfied?
Where do I find my wealth?
Will it always be like this,
Scared gawking at the distance?

Finding You means everything
Everything means now
Fragile is the will
Consumed in the past
Bothered is the state of mind
Where nothing lasts
Needing some other proof
Waiting for some different view
But Your word is all I need

Take all the doubt
The distractions that impede
The praises I still will shout
There is no sense living compromised or indecisive

Take all the fears, frozen in their place
The source of my greed
In every self defense
Come near; let Your word be spoken
Here in this moment

Paint Creek

Empty from a wince, a fresh stream
Underneath a new bridge
Eyes on a river, they melt into one
If what shrugs be the silence, its true
Everything You point towards
Alas there were clues
But in planting them,
Lord we become shaken
A little renown by the thought and its inception
You're sinking in
So wait, when You are with us
There are no secrets that in this light couldn't prove
We are worthy to be as You might
Yes wait my friend and listen
Through the bend a ripple
Flowing through a life
So simple

Tomorrow

Stay with me, insist the truth, instill my life
For it's Your voice that pulls me here, out of time
As it brightens, that way into the familiar
Everything in space screams
There's a future
But whatever is tomorrow
Won't be the chase today

For it's a different fuel that finds the flame
A simple course that claims today
And while You have me here, Lord
Far from want or any idle need
There are no cares stranger to my passion
As my will carries with it the prompting of the spirit's desire
To bring me home to peace, all the while
I need You now, let everything wait
Be my wisdom, be my strength

To Teach

Knots and needles
Broken boughs bending
Hear the passage of Your word
Trembling leaves are burdened
By your twist and turn
Steady by me here
Teach me, I will listen
For this is the truth
Drawn down my defenses
Yes, you know why we're here
Urge us gently
Become everything we rely on
Take us from the moment we know
Into the lifetime where we teach
But keep on learning
Like breeze in the calm
Grab our attention
Heighten our senses to thy true word
Come, Holy Spirit, Come

Me and You

See my vision set it straight
See the envelope turn, nothing erased
There's the point, I am here to make you see the life I have intended
Pure hearts set upon their God
There is nothing else, there is nothing more
Love and know I am near
Live in abundance
Live, see that nothing exists or persists apart from the truth
I am with you
And none of what you've seen or been through
Was intended to damn you or make you oblivious
I love you, though at times it hurts and it makes your brain wonder
But I don't cease, I am always beginning
And I am not through until
You see there are no straight lines in this path
There's just me and you
And there is no difference its just me and you
(Praise be to God)

From the Valley

From the valley
Raising my eyes till they meet the horizon
No longer afraid
Clouds, passing storms that choked the light
I see the chasm dead to right over the hills
This is where the chains get left behind

All the proofs that had me frightened
Of my own self, there are rested
The patented lies, of traction, of ties
It is by their spite that breeds confusion
Slurring my step on the oppressive floor
Ribbons of thunder channel through the hollows
But I am no longer afraid

Echoes, memories/states of being/what was past
Invite me to stay
Only to be spoiled in their remains
Freedom is the shaft of light racing up the foothills
For I have waited for this day and the promise to believe
Seeing all that is perfect,
Hope it reaches me
Rising from the valley

By Your Waters

Set ablaze, shake the dawn
By Your waters
Through the expanse of Your heart,
Call me home
Make Your mark
Define where I am
Ripples set free, run asunder
Hear me all and all

This is not yesterday
Across a wave calling back
Or a muse running down the same track
For when the mist covers the hillside
You are free
When the trees are still
Broken in by Your light
There You speak

It's the horizon that expands
Far beyond where I am going
As the dream seizes
The best You'd have of me
Tension is a breeze calling, disturbing a still lake
Oh, I hear the Creator cry, "Good Morning!"

Even as I am

Even as I am staring out at the playground,
It's nothing, no noise from in here.
The glass windows I shed,
And I know if seeing You as real,
Makes the sense it could,
In front of the elliptical transfusion,
This is the hour,
We are alive,
What noise is now made makes the prophets disappear
Into the shadows of angel's wings.
But I hear the sun warm the grass,
And the excitement of all that lasts.
Hiding behind the outwash, the isolated pillars of entropy,
Feelings that now bleed into suggestions of what wasn't spent:
Fuel emancipated from lips poised in God's Praise
Grey mottled avenues, of winds that spread light
From the blue opaque engine,
Driving noble cast shadows
Onto the likelihood you know what you've been given

The Encouragement

I'm not trying to humiliate you, but the road is long
You've only just begun believing
And what I see in you is far beyond what you see in the mirror
Everything that has become these mountains
Everything that you know to be true
They are no match, you will overcome them all

The task maybe daunting, and the way
Unnatural to the way you've been living
But I am here, and I will be with you, always
Remember not that those cliffs are so high
And that the challenges are great
Do not fear for in the end
You'll cast every stone to the sea
You'll walk in meadows and fields teeming with light
Know that I am your God
Through everlasting life

Anew

Empty me
Pour out every blessing
Achieve as You will
Oh, Father
So, as I have believed
This is Your life unending
Take it, renew it now
Everything is waiting

Be it blessed by intent
From a life spared from any regret
Live in me now
Soul secure, spirit willing
Drawn me from within
Until nothing wasted
Is left behind/
Swallowed in a grave

This is my all
No more wishing I was somewhere else
No more tangled, misspent thoughts
Dreaming I was someone else
All I live for begins and ends with You
You are ever teaching
Reaching,
Making me anew

The Winter of the Soul

This isn't real
As strong as I feel
What do you really know?
Words become then they go
Who can bridge the gap along the path of understanding?
What is and evermore shall be?
This is the winter of the soul
Where have the clouds erased the shadows
And visible is the call home
Thought is loosed from knots of attrition
Snow leads upon the trails as we follow
Whence was the way we haven't strayed
It's just a season trying not to freeze in one place

Hold on my Heart

Hold on my heart
There you go supposing
Well I don't know
If you have some answers,
Won't you tell me?
And if you know the way,
Oh, here we go?

Set upon a course
For your survival
You've entertained the days
But what still remains?
Educated guesses plant
A mountain of suggestion:
Lord why are You distant?

Who are You a king,
And You know right from wrong?
I am just a child, I concede
I will never know it all
Presence makes its plea
All I am
Waiting to receive

Call unto me
Is it everything?
It is everything
From basic need
To all I can't see
Well You are the Lord of all
You have carried me thus far
Hold on my heart

Home

You're the answer
You're the destination
A brooding point of commonality
Across this finished race
We want to be home

Nothing else satisfies
Recharges the mind
Instills the soul
And habours love
Quite like home

Everything is secondary
Be it money
Be it fame
Be it a whirlwind tour across the world
Nothing gravitates, nothing is anticipated
Just like home

What is it that makes us believe in such a place?
What is it that pushes us further
Past all exhaustion and strife?
Oh, one day we will be home

For it's more than a country
A roof over your head
A place to party, a place to crash
It's where love grows
And it sends us forth
Deeper still, until we get there
We will always long for home

The Wonder of a Dream

She wants to see the tears in my eyes
And the smile that brings them down to earth
Crystal clear was the dream they beckoned
From far beyond what we could even fathom

Everything impossible stretches its hands
To the God that doesn't disappoint
But perhaps you don't see the picture
Or you listen to the scorn of the nay-saying chorus

They are always on time, never in tune
We are blessed with the grace that fills our days
Even though the steps taken may have been painful
And the refrain keeps telling you: You'll never make it
But we know even as we stand;

The first step takes the longest
Weeks, Months, years
And it meets with the heaviest resistance
As the greatest of foes are plotting, counting on your retreat
But be brave knowing the next step
Needs only a second's worth of instruction
Trust becomes the way that through His endless imagination
We are brought up into the wonder of a dream
That His will, His plan, His timing can only fulfill

Sensation

Wince, tear my eyes from the crest
You are building, taking something away
If you knew sunshine
If you knew the haze still blurs the burning in my eyes

Reach out and see there is something left
Life cascading, curling ribbons extend
Desire turns to the taste when I met you
Not that joy knew anything different
This is where it all begins
To follow You is to know of You
It is not enough

We meet in a perfection of sensation
In time bridged and melted away
The sting of effort exposed in the coolness
A bath releasing the tension
Of life immersed, blessed
More than I know
There you roll,
Washing over me

In the Interest of Time

Cornered
Indebted to You only
Race the thought that (looks up)
And is still
Standing still
Laugh
Transplant(dumb mockery)
Oh, time
The very bother
And traction of life
You seem so sticking
To the point
You never leave me
Devalued
Is your stock still rising?
Roll over and let me know
That when I get there
You were at the very least:
Interest(ing)

The Living Will

Every hesitation tells me something
If opinions turn into options, more or less revealed
You can speak clearly
But the barrier of understanding shifts the spirits within me
Yes, something moves as the untrained become trained?

I look and its not the same world
When we started this walk
Speech is a quiet thought, dancing
I hear everything but the words become unglued
In the presence of the wind

For in the direction of the process there is no transient calling
That neither devises the next step nor befriends a second guess
So that in the wrestling of its purpose
I wonder:

Does serving You lead part of me to forsake what You already told me?
Some things we chase blind in broad daylight
Bound in intention, serving our appeals
What has left me weary to a fault
Is not the proof that urges me on
No we have just begun
To share a will

Right on Time

You are always---breaking through the static
Sifting through the feedback
I know I am home
You make your way to the forefront
And You renew my mind
It's like You are calling me
Even though I'm not so sure
But in everything that's gone on
You breathe in lasting peace

I am in You because You never compromised
I love You because You liberated my life
And when everything else is breaking up
You're the voice that I cannot leave behind
Your very word fuels me and lets me know:
You are right on time

Details and All

Whatever the means,
The Way will show you
Whatever the cost, it wasn't yours to choose
Submission to your own understanding
Breeds bitter doubt
Into the insecurity of what you haven't figured out
"But everything you got going, kid
Is mine don't you waste it"

Finished is a glossy term for polished
As closure isn't all it should seem to be
On this side of eternity
Screaming is your self to please
Because now you don't get it, and that's alright
But just love the one who set you up
And you'll no longer deny
Say; Lord, "have it your way"
So you'll know the fruit, the truth and the believing
Is to trust, details and all

The Trust Fall

And as I have reached the point
Tipping back
Where the silence isn't offering the solace
After muttering under my breath
Into open space, unsure
It's like this when I miss You
And I feel needy
How do I give that up?

Its not the first time I waged for this to be
I just want to be sure again
But the more I wait,
I suffocate
And the more I'm sure that you're waiting
Doesn't make it all make sense to me
But I don't even know
Lord, I just don't know why
Do I have to let go?
Do I have to let go?
What happens, if I let go?

Clay

Touchdown, take it back
Change your mind
You're like a freight train
Running away from the track

He takes your life
And it breaks it
He's the master of time
And He shapes you back to the point
Where you can see
He's totally right

You couldn't carry on/bear the weight
Shaped to hold more
Now you've been deeply changed
Down to the very core

Molded, intent fully noticed
Master, keep pushing/keep pulling
Let the old be fashioned new
Like into something worthy,
Oh, we're touched by You

From the Water's Edge

As frightened bait is torn away by the wind
I keep talking to you in the efforts that you'll give in
Some say the shallow waters confuse and then drown
All of complacency,
It soon turns into whispers all around
Remind me of how this lesson makes believers of men
I swear that if you let go its not like it should have been

Into this primacy of wonder you age,
Your senses bear the world until you become lost
Feel the sand scuttle under your feet,
You can move officially beyond the waves tossed?

I want to hold onto you forever,
Sacrifice beside the days the years
To know you as you have to grow
But you must do more than walk through these waters that flow
God must teach you of the horizons
That insist on belief beyond what we feel
It's somewhere deeper,
And as soon as you get there you'll ask me is it real?

The Dream of Winter

The preparation leads you to knots
Still camouflaged is the dream on the horizon
Leaving you weeping as soon the sun disappears
Thinking it out, thinking aloud
The invisible will still grow spots
Lo, behold you can wake me
Now I am listening
In a manner, a sense I am asking
Something here reminds me of a memory
That follows a forecast and yet achieves its own destiny
It's the cold night that leaves comfort second-guessing
Expectancy grabs a hold of everything
Breaks the chains you don't have to wear
Letting you enjoy the winter, maybe this year

The Extension of Grace

There is something so subtle that stakes the difference
Between the balance of your life and its cold reflection
I am stood still by the shadow your entrance creates
Imposed is the dawn to your expansive reveille
But now you are poised and you just slide away
Too graceful to tumble into something that isn't you

Expecting a Blessing

When a thought chased a dream
Looking for a place to hide
Running from the shadows' plight
I wasn't with the train it wrecked
Nor did I carefully place my bets
Hoping to win at the sweepstakes

But has time weighed in?
Bringing dust and its inevitability:
Allergies and a mind numbed to mush
Take me from this winter,
Know that even if I planned to escape
I would rather be tied to a blessing, only patience provides,
Sure of an answer--Born of Your light

Take me Home (Not so Fast)

Jesus take me home, he said
It's the difference now my life has meant
Waiting for a son
Father, please forgive me
For I knew not where to start or to end
Save the offering of my pen
Halleluiah, take my now

For when the light shines in his eyes
I am ready
Lord, take me home
For all the music has stopped
And I cannot go on
Praying for another word, another song
And the days are long
And if its not coming,
Am I done, is that all?

No, this is not my plight
Or the sanction on my life
As the years haven't played out this desire for my life
I am young
For take me to the place where I am exhausted
And I cannot give any more
Take me to the limit
Where I can still shout for You in the middle of the fight
We are winning; we are taking on new ground
Don't let it end, Lord
Keep feeding me Your Holy Spirit, Your design
I'm standing armor and all
Just one more song that lifts Your people
Just one more day to answer Your call

Faith

"Faith is not believing the truth,
By succeedingly, passively, awaiting its proof,
We walk in it"

In the light of what you've shown me
In this place, so like a movie
There goes the scenes I've seen before
And the dream I've seized once more

From here I've glimpsed the Promised Land
And seen this future close at hand
But I want more than visions from the mountaintop
For spared is the fruit of its bearing lost
I want to walk in it

I want to walk in every promise you've placed in my heart
To know the completeness, I have dreamt from afar
I want to walk in with courage
And displace every fear
To be with you Father
And know you are near

Silence Speaks

Silence strike a pose
Catch me thinking:
Is it you again?
I just want to believe
That if you are somehow along for the same ride
Teach me something
Talk me down

Well I am sure as in otherwise
Lasting, long enough
Past charades, and disguises
Assuming the long view
Resting safely in the driver's seat,
Only now I'm lost for words

An Invitation

Even in this small room I have lost my place
Lord I reach out my hand, for You to show me the way
Things have to be different now,
For I have been consumed
Living in the shadows of a substandard dream
I'm sure it is not coming from You

For it seems like eternity I have waited for You to enter this room
Break down these doors,
To enlighten this space where I'll no longer live
Cause from now on I'll believe in something more,
I'll respect all You have to give
Knowing just where You extend your kingdom,
Well it never end

In a sense I feel you are already here:
Yes, every moment its You that matters
Move my mouth to speak of Your wisdom,
Come to me in these desperate hours
I want to be Your messenger,
I live to defend Your holy name and I want to do You right

It is Time

What gives weight to a burden,
Despair to the downtrodden?
For in this darkness
Is the force-fed apathy
But they have not seen the likes of me and you

For this is my generation, says the Lord
You are my people, hungry for my Word
For lo, you have waited and you will be fed
You will be bold and see me raise the dead
No one has seen the passion I have instilled in you

Yes, you are my people
In me you reside
In me may your thoughts remain,
Your hands to heal,
My heart to be revealed to a hurting world
Let no one be forsaken
It is time
Oh, it is time

Song of the Delivered

In the midst of my troubles
I will pour out my heart in praise
Dare I run out of breath
And I can no longer speak,
For my heart, my soul,
It cries out for the Lord
Because He is good
And He has saved me

I will sing to the Lord in purpose-filled tones
With every aching of my spirit,
He hears me now
His mercy is surely urgent
As with grace comes the holding of His care
In Him, I no longer stand alone
And these words will no longer be trapped inside of me
Lord you reach me, You pour out Your Love
You've proven Your greatness time and again
And I am honored to witness and minister
All because you've brought Your Son Jesus into my life

Because He has healed me and I look forward
I don't look back at time misspent
For as I know Your Spirit is within me, You teach me
You are always reaching for me
May You find in me a servant
Worthy to follow you
Even though I am so undeserving

The Risen Son

Wait until the encompassing retreat, fear intends on the break of dawn
Drawn always to the brink of eternal understanding
The clouds that where cobalt and gray have turned to mellow hot pink
While the distinct remnants of night cling to the breath of cosmic wind
Across the foothills the flock stirs
Under the guise of successful watchmen
Free to roam, but imposed by the rocky ground
To where the ends of life meet
These sheep are intent to be defined by their master
To understand the totem, **living** water must lay inherent in stone
Pebbles lay only be scattered in the haste of those who are hungry
Even within the ancient soil comes the reinforcement:
The Risen Son keeps watch over the quick and the dead

A Brilliant Sky

For once there was a brilliant sky
So rich it could be written as a song
And once there came the kind of love and trust
That couldn't be explained with chosen words
It's in some photo-taken memory
How the stills are now longer silenced
As the spirit ripples in waves to change us
Now all I see is your beauty
It's like how God intended it to be
There is more to us than thoughts of kindness
For the hungry trails that were traced
In each of our eyes have found peace here
Trust in our Lord has journeyed us
Through the expanses of our loving hearts
What breathes through us is the play of our faith,
Into the promise of love, forever

April's River

Here the river is wide
Swelling banks and borders
I'm lost is space
Needing to remember why it is you
But there's no tempting of fate,
That flows by unsettled, unresolved
Beauty casts its reflection on the surface
Swarming in life
For this fulfilled is the bridge between me and you
As the sky emblazoned drifts colors
Flowing from the edges of space into another life
Guided by inquiry
From its conception standing in place
A dream is locked up in consequences
But something here remains unspoiled
And welcomes a breeze
To shake a portrait far from being still

Always on Time

The stiles keep spinning
None my eyes too forgiving
In a war with shadows and light
Seeing everything succumb to the highlight reel
Ever dancing--taking me in
But is it You that are moving,
As I am the one standing still?

Film breathes in life then it forms
Creating molds cast in time
Actors become relevant the more you rewind
Can we start over?
I don't want to go,
Do I have to go?
Is this the about-face of the undertow?

By faith, know where you are headed
Smile sink in, there that's better
No, you are not standing still
What revolves around you are not the stars of someone else's plot
They are your own, learn and live with them
Live, change, let go,
Yes, you will shine
Trust you are always on time

Lost

I know there is meaning beyond the definition
When you are hurt and you need to be heard
Everyone's looking but you are not taking the same road
Everything's stinking and yes you're feeling so old

We keep on picking it up
To lay it down
We keep on picking it up
Just to lay it down again
You'd take the upside
If you knew it would get you by
You'd make the right turn
If it could buy you the time

There's no easy way through
When all your tears keep on building
A tide that rolls in
And covers the best of your sight
But He hears you
And blink, child,
You'll never be lost
Let His word sink in
And blink, child
You'll never be lost

From the Clouds

Everything of value
All that is stored in the heavens must come down
But what on earth are we saving for?
Possessions that exhaust,
Feelings that subside,
Oh, but in time what remains?

For do the clouds get tired?
No,
They change their shape
And head to the horizon of another man's dream
As was purchased,
So as it is:
The light poured through
Shines for His glory
Now that darkness no longer has another foothold in another mind,
Dare another life

This is the move of a genius
No thought, no breath be wasted
Everything passes, persists on His watch
Nothing is greater than the passion of our creator
Yes, taking in step, in discretion
Time and space
At the hands of the master

For every gift
Every dream fathomed
Is His to own, His to share
So from the heavens expect this much:
His love, His touch, His light
Is ours for eternity
Everything you complete shall be His
Like it always
Peace

The Extension of You

For what lives in fear
Cannot be freedom
As time insures the safest place
For life to become clear
Don't let me go

Talk/Break into this mind
Purpose everything
Have me always resting completely in Your arms
Love, can you teach me?
Love ever needing
I want life, where at the end of who I am
Is the extension of You, the part that keeps growing

I no longer want plans or the truth solely as I want them to be
I want You
To know Your purpose, though it takes time
To see Your vision, because I cannot even dream that far
And on the way
Lord, I'll need Your grace, because I know I make mistakes

Epiphany

Down to being daring
The discipline moves you forward
Golden is the motive traced in a clearinghouse
Set free at Godspeed

Know that in today is sprung all that could be endeavored
From tomorrow's questioned plight
Oh, one breakthrough at a time
Lost sheep get caught in your mind

Everything equates to the effort
Everything gestured from strife
No, what is bargained for is priceless
Passed by is the process:

The same truth is drawn from better consequences
Belief exhumes the ever after
When all at once is the sense,
Could it have come any sooner?

Emmanuel

A hint
Perfect place
Order
A plan so devised and simple
Born today
Everything has become so wrapped in You
How obscure
Oh, little town
Now you are laid in swaddling clothes
In the throes, of a manger
But alive, yes alive
Blessed, in whose eyes
Compassion never stumbles
And everything touched
Finds wholeness, finds peace
To hope in life anew
Such was formed the heart of a servant
Forever, the lion and the lamb
Who rules in love
And whose promises forever stand
What a blessed joy
First born, divine
Just a little baby boy

In the Morning

Stars fade into the morning sun
As gravity assumes and plays upon the horizon
Another day has begun
From where dust treads on the bare feet
Waiting seeks closure on another day's dream
Look out--look within
Something moves across the surface
Wipe the tear from the grin
Eyes flood in joy
Praise races from this heart, from this soul
Oh, what cannot be contained
The impossible, where the spirit reigns
Forevermore is the reason still living in today
Glory wages into glory
Promises sealed in the morning

Blue

Underneath is a grain of sand
Within is the home I long for
Above are the stars disguised in an atmosphere
Tempting to keep things blue
No, is this as close as I get today?
Just another wave at the shoreline
A place dancing on the ring of fire
Or am I attempting something greater?
Leading, pretending to start swimming
One stroke, two, just a start that I cannot finish
But oh, this is good enough, today
To not be pulled by an undertow's submission
A fate not deserved, designed for this day
Oh, there is something, beyond the horizon of blue

Out on a Plane

Radiant
Hold nothing back
Everything keeps waiting for a sign
A token to redeem a better pasture not spoiled in mottled earth
For you cannot steal cobblestones from street corners
Or secure breath not taken in thin air
As to leave you compromised down the same road

Awaken what the fool says is dead
Capture what the soul needs to prosper
Yes, the extension of life
Release what is yours
Light, purity of life
Draw forth, champion Son's delight

The Harbour of Expectation

Here in the harbour of expectation
The outlook is constantly shifting
At first I am glad I am sealed
But then I know I am caught
Trapped by my own definitions
Surrogate lies and ammunition
Amongst/between
I just feel sunk

For the bar is high as the tide is high
When at first everything just disappoints
And I cannot get out of here on time
Every dream plays about the horizon
Then is cast in doubt

I'm afraid that I will never get out of the harbour
And I am so sick of trying
Everything I push, pushes back harder
I give up trying to figure it out
I wonder, examining for the answer
Knowing all too well:
I must have forgot to pull up the anchor

Athena

I rest in the shadow cast
From the pedestal
All I can do is wrap my arms
Around the base of understanding
Knowing all too well I'm ill-equipped
To reach such heights
As long as I'm beneath her
I cannot feel the warmth of true light

Some say I'm just confused
That I'll never sense the truth
Or bask in the creation of its proof
As I strain to reach her toes
They gleam in sufficient light, but I suppose
Odds are, what I think of her will never be true
And as I try to break from her incessant pull
I wonder if she sees me, is that a wink,
No, I must have been deceived

The Last Sacrifice

What have I left to hold onto?
No shame, no indifference?
Just the power of a vision
And a stepwise plan
Far above the horizon
Or the competency of man
I see smoke signals and the gathering dust
Shaken by the brunt of used hands
Time has become the fulfilling gesture raised on an altar

Consumed is the landscape
Where borrowed ideals become idols
Sacrificed to our egos
To the profit of none
I don't want to breathe in any more of these charred remains
Promises unspoken to the death
Bones remain and are scattered to mark the ground
Where forgotten is not the sacrifice
Its power supplanted by the pursuit of the living God

Weaving

There is something here
Past all I want to see
Or everything I claim to be
Slip through the lie of my reflection
Tease away thoughts that leave me so
Effortless, at first it was easy
But where is Your heart?
Pulling at strings
Looms still upon Your weaving
Your heart and mine
Running, stumbling at the words
Posing new questions
Answers intact, ample by and by
To double-back
Yes, remind me
How this becomes the invention
Of a present state of mind?

Get on With the Lord

There's a proof waiting past desire
There's a moment, amassed looking for hire
Take it in/call yourself ready
By the time takes,
Evolves into a memory
You cannot devise
You cannot divide from the truth
Combat, Contain/ release tomorrow
Reach in/pull back
There ain't nothing willed and asked for that you'll ever lack
Look forward, be sure
Take the time/turn it over
Get on with the Lord

Redwood

Awe, to be carried to such height
Not to be let go of
But to wonder
In a soaring trance a light, a vision
Not formed in effort
Or rooted without a cause
Needles, spires in defense reaching to the point
Where is the rise of destiny
And something so grand
When you can't face the shadows you make
You're briefed by another breeze
As everything rests below teased but to reach out
You are postured by something this earth still shapes
By sight alone you won't be torn down
To fathom the distance you've left to create
Not an extension burned down,
But spared the injury
Released from the nurturing bed
Flourishing through time instead

Beyond the Shore

What is lead?
Why can I not follow You this time?
The sea is left at my feet
It wishes to go no further
As the horizon shifts slightly
I can only discern the plan:
What is the definition of my life,
Amongst the wager of the current?

As I take on water, I choose to not be distracted
Neither by the wind
Or (deeper then) the wake I assume
Weeds break apart,
Their forgiveness allows me to move
For to proceed is to know something more than myself
Yes, to be defined by His likeness
Bears the ultimate proof

I look around and see that I am afloat
Resolute of His will
Consumed in the infinite
I am drawn deeper still
Remind me why it is so demanding:

Life's mystery is carried beyond the tides
And it will tell you:
The view is free from the beach
But the only life worth a mention
Is the one that is drawn into God's intention

Exposed

Exposed is the shoreline
The cliffs of white
Strong is the prevailing wind
That lays the beach below
There's nowhere to hide

Once time sheds this morsel of rock
To the depths and the raging sea
No longer can I be says the soul
Stripped away by degrees are the scales
And the coarseness surrounding my heart
The rock and the impenetrable layers
That the years made in haste

Oh, that I am wise enough now
To welcome the wind,
Let it find my heart, and know its end
So I can be as the sand,
Rolling in the tides

Here to Stay

Well I know what broken is
And the one who makes us whole again
When I am not sure there is a way
His truth refutes the darkest day

Wading through the waves of sorrow
Is the hope that bears tomorrow
Where there are dreams that do take flight
Bought and paid for by His life

For I have felt the bitter chill
While all the while my heart needed filled
Praying fore the season's change
But, alas my Lord You are here to stay

In His Hands

You've always had the winning hand
Don't fold,
Don't cash it in
Where there are no re-deals
You're apt to keep silent,
And wherever there's doubt
You'd figure out that someone else's got it better
And why am even in this, this far?

There are times when you squeem
There are times when you'd rather not keep it to yourself
But every fiber of your being is His
And He doesn't make junk
He doesn't even lose
Trust
He's got you covered
Ease into the joy that is yours
And be reminded destiny is in His hands

Of Another Day's Dream

It is here every time---this is hopeless
But what do I know?
Same thought cries, "Foul"
And yet something deeper sees a free range
Where all the things taken for granted/
All seeds that have been sown
Agitate the soil/And need time to grow

Discernment becomes the welcome thought
Trouble passes by approved on the same lot
This is where you glean and make the difference
To welcome the indeed from the essence
For what you see as nothing
May just be evidence
Of another day's dream

One Move

Fleeting
That's all it's intended to be
Wonder, where have you gone?
A New Day
Tell me it's a new day

I know this wasn't meant to last
But I keep holding on as if there's something more
There always is…
That I don't get, that seems to pass

Yes, there's one way
Only one way
It's just I'm all out of options
Like more would make me wealthy

No, just one move
That's all I ask for
A break
Something that says I've been waiting for
The right thing, Lord

On the Radar

Stolen from the thin air
I found my spirit
So spun from the dust
I recognized my life
With every word I wrought an explanation
And with every breath in silence I assumed the truth
Nothing is missing
Not a question
Not a cause
Or the effect of perfection
The need for applause

It is deafening what's been thrown down from the heights
How light splits the darkness as the heavens collide
So aware is the earth
It takes a hold of my wonder
How it shakes,
Oh how I run for cover
You chase the pressure
Soon the pressure drops

All of this thunder
Oh, that it might rain
But this is all in season
Sure, let it pass unrestrained
Whatever it wills;
Stubborn, don't--
Just let it be
Everything keeps calling from the echoes on my knees

The Battlefield

I have seen the battlefield
And the swarms of fighting entities
They clash, the mount up
As they have one purpose:
To vanquish the promised/
To trample the chosen
But have seen the Lord
I have seen Him weave through the legion,
Unscathed
I have seen Him touch the very center of the enemy
And He has torn him down
This is what He has done for you
His beloved
For You above all know:
It is finished
Claim what is rightfully yours
Hallelujah, praise His name

Leading The Blind

Is there something You want from me?
Not that I've freely given
Or have solely departed
Pride if you are in here, trying to make it another round
Faith, the lack of you, are you tying me down?

Tell me there's more
More of You, less of the rest of what I call myself
This cannot be as far as we go
Its too much, there's too much, heavens no

I don't have to see everything
I'll leave that to You
And what I long to believe
Isn't what You've given me already
I want one thing:
A sure next step
Seen, unseen, just confident

The Harvest Song

He wants more than what He put in
He's not satisfied getting what he got last year
And there's a reason, we cannot be the same
There's a season, for us to bring it in once again
Talents rain, to be purposed
Love abounds and is fulfilled,
Overflows the storehouses once again
Delight showers on the forgiven
While we sow, not knowing
All that is to be told
It's the harvest, let us rejoice
Gather in the goodness that has been promised
Sing praise, for our Father is good
Thanksgiving is upon us
Oh, He is so good

Victory

I believe in the victory
Before the battle is fought
I believe in the destiny
Paid for and bought
For in the end everything will bow to You, oh, Lord
And nothing escapes Your presence, unchanged

You are the promise fulfilled
You are the love everlasting
And the reason I keep leaning on Your Word
You heal the broke-hearted
You renew our minds
In everything upon everything
You are present, You're alive

Thank you for this life
Though the work isn't done
Thank you for Your precious Holy Spirit
My guide, the journey's just begun
Master Jesus, You've filled my life
I respond, I breathe in new life because you bought me with a price
Father, the author of all, perfect love
You believed in me right from the beginning
How awesome, how beautiful is all the work of Your hands
Halleluiah, You are King

For The Privileged

How can I say that I am poor,
When I have clean clothes on my bed?
How can I say I am hungry,
When I have leftovers to eat?
How can I say I am persecuted,
When its KJV or NIV?

This is a life spoiled in riches
Yet we somehow have room to complain
We have choices: houses of worship, and freedom of worship
And no one questions, we are free?
Humbled, let us be humble
Let us realize in the vastness and in luxury
We stand blinded to the reality
That a different world exists only a few miles away

This is the whole world Christ died for
We are called to be responsible
In that our lives be ones lived in the service of our creator
And that we may find the strength that is freely given
To transform lives indebted through His purpose
As we become thoroughly committed servants
Wholly in need

Autumn Leaves December

What is the illusion that baits me to stray
From staring undisturbed at the fallen leaves?
For it's the amber shades of a late evolving season
Across the many miles to what feels like home
Yeah, it's a month or so too late

But now that I see,
Will it ever be the same?
No, still there are eyes
They will never forget you
Soon they will stare at what is left
The patience applied pursuant of truth
From here you will see it pass by
Yes, you will see it without fail

But I cannot tell its meaning from true life
True life from its separate remains
Cornered and scared
Offered in truce, yet afraid to be spoken
Alive, yet we're slowly taken
By the chill it leaves behind

Forward

I am sick of hanging onto myself
I'm a new man
I am not a shadow or reminder of my former self
I'm a new man
For endowed in Christ, I am nothing less
And what I depend on, only You Lord, is my need

I cannot make the wake push me forward
Nor can I trust that it is my reason for being
Nothing thrust from the weight I assume of myself
Moves me forward
No, when your Spirit reigns over me
A nuance of truth is consumed, is delivered

This is the fresh light, and I won't leave it
This is the fresh trail and Lord I believe it
Awe is for everything
Your thoughts and the love You give me
Beyond my understanding
Holding onto the might by which You saved me

An Inch

I wanted a mile
But all I got was an inch
You talk, we talk
You slip by me
A cooling stream
Knee-deep forgiving
Whatever I meant when I spoke
Words trailed off, fingers grew cold
Yes, You are past me
Thorough, beyond, brave, interceding
You are potent as You have proven
In even the least of what I can hold
Clarity takes a step forward
Rustles the pebbles
Clouds the next step
Wait as time refreshes/
Provides unto everything
A lift for an expectant heart,
Now I look up, smile its progress
If even for an inch

Present

When you predicate the expectation
Well, there is none
But if it's about a simple nudge
A passion to know your worth
Then it's in the believing
That my being longs so

Persistently awake beside what are only dreams
Their shape/transparency cannot compare to what is here now
Because it is here where I meet You
And nothing is as important
No noise, no trouble
No perspiration of thought
Only You I welcome
In every bit of Your reign
You fit me in

Through the Storms

I was laid in the shadows of some consequence
It took me from the light I knew
Yes, into this world I withdrew
Not knowing if I'd make it back
Considering I was way off track
There has got to be a message
In all means a passage

No, I do not want to be here
No, I have to make that clear(through a way a cannot see)
But I know my Savior will lead me
Back to the place where I will not feel alone
Where I can see a life, a promise to hold
This is what I hope for
A dream, a life through the storms

Better Than The Hype

Oh, we knew You were coming
But we didn't know why
Rumors fell apart
Our hopes went there and died
As we waited for You to start some war
So to deliver us all,
Captive in our hearts

We know You walked in our midst
As we're bound by Your Word
Caught in your presence
Nothing remains the same
So soon we wanted to hail You as king
But You forsook every crown
'cept the one of thorns
Lord, we know You're still living
No, our lives can't deny
Spirit come and speak
Let there be no question
Pour yourself onto this generation
Beyond our comprehension
So beyond our belief

But You're better than the hype
Or what we've known as glory
It's through your perfect passion
Your purpose is always
Love before pride, always on time

You're the one
The only one
Whose love is better than the hype

The One and Only Way

Your voice travels quickly across the dark room
Unbent by florescent light and its defiant purpose
What has evolved in an unmastered test?
Your only critic seems to be the loose floorboards
Responding to your unsure posture
The room is dimensionless, as you extend yourself slowly
You lose track of where you've been
And there's got to be a door a window to the outside
Yet the path was so discrete, now there's nothing to left remind you
Time is of no essence, trapped only by your attention
As where you've been doesn't tell you where to go
Guidance, is it something concrete?
Exhausted in a room without end
You fall to your knees, observant of the one and only way

From the Crowd

Why'd you want to fail a million times,
Just to buy the time to get it right?
Somewhere has something
Another way of dreaming
That this could be the life?

Wake me (So no longer sleeping)
Trust me (All there is to needing)
Lead me (Built upon believing)
For everything paled from perfect
Chiming in the choice key
Wallowed in the wrong voice
Ends up getting there, slowly by degrees

And the price that has been binding
Not the very shade of a crisis
Is the living of the choicest sound
Getting there, yeah
A poised piece from the crowd

Out of Your Shell

Leaving before hello sunk in
For I don't know
Is this freedom?
But this how your life will begin
In this time I look up at the full-length mirror
Shining both ways
And I see the proof that none of our words
Fell on deaf ears, expired not for the thought
I am moving too, just bearing the middle ground

In what you ask for patience provides
Every bit a possession shared into belief
For a season
To have your needs met
So that you'll never forget
Blessing is all that I can give to you
May the richness of your faith
And the absolute beauty of your being
Triumph over any darkness or fear that tries to assail you
Victory, sweet victory
Life, fullness, simplicity

Sculpted

What is left to be done?
Carve the impossible from the rock?
Listen in, brace the hammer
Across the fault line the weight falls off
Everything that means anything
Is driven with time and prayer, steadied hands

If being was as easy to create we'd be done long ago
But something just grows
Is it love, a perception that we are molded
Placed on a path, shaken from the parent material
And grasped, polished in petitions tears
Perhaps wisdom never cheats her cousin patience
And we're just waiting for another chip off the block

Jacob's Well

You don't have to like me
But I know where you've been
You don't have to compromise
What I offer you'll never find
Racing through what you thought of when
Or living from a source of regret

This is where the word quenches thirst
And all the wandering ceases
I am the oasis that never runs dry
I am the hope you long for when you through with another guy
Wells run deep and the water glistens
Pour it out, but listen:

I can only satisfy
What your soul, your spirit surely need
I am all there is, look no further
I am living water

Good Morning

Silence breaks upon the dawn
And you are listening
Shaken/
Awakened by its new song
Defining the breadth of your attention:

Come see, come breathe
With arms raised gather the strength
Its your morning, your morning
Purchased at an expense
So you no longer need to stumble
Rest, be assured,
That as soon as yesterday became today
You had decided--
And as much as decisions need time
They have been arrested
And held captive

Dreams
Real as in waking
Have become but floating captions
Never to be read into common sense
Nor headed in any direction, no less
They've been clean slated by a repercussion
Breathed through a yawn
And they'll persists unto the awakening of life
Where alas, an opening of a door
There you've seen the light,
And yes, you want more

The Way

To wander in the fog
Short-sighted
Where akin to the meaning of distress
Braves the better of hope obscured
Eyes turn and the wander
Are they lost?

For the way out is cut through time
In layers, aberrations
Ghosts afraid of light
Pulling free from the horizon
So wait and the way is sure
Leveraging the mind plays down the consequence
That makes every trial bigger than it ought to be

Footholds, footprints
Nothing unplanned
Nothing amiss
Ah, veil is lifting
The way past your eyes

Refreshed (On the Road)

Tears of rain fell from wrinkled clouds
An old day loves its daughter
A new trail left to ponder:
Are we getting there?
See how we left the certainty
Then drew a line however briefly in our minds
We're done with the waiting, and not backing up
It's not how we'll stay fulfilled in the dust
Or cornered in our own trust

The rain soaks in deeper
Every bit the cowards they'd say
But to pick up is where we left off
Believing there was more to existence
Yes there's more to go the distance
See the blacktop see what is left of the rain
Somehow the steam hovers gently to be torn
Picked up by the wind sweeping
By a breeze so warm

The Fire

Every fire has a way of burning still
Despite what the darkness tries to conceal
Passion propels His presence
And is birthed into this dimension

What you see is the power
No one can snuff out
Every dream that's created
Nothing is wasted
Unto the belief and the reason you are still burning:

Because there in His eyes, He sees tomorrow
And there's fuel for the flame
May the spirit lead you on
So that you remain
A light that fuels everyone

I am Cleansed

I breathe in the silence
I live in the air, clear
What are gone are the voices
Those forces of disrepair
They never moved me anywhere
Anywhere of my need

Where did they come from?
They are gone
For I've fought against every stronghold
Cast down every fear
Till you oh, Lord were left
Because it's for always
Your word against all the lies
And I've heard them all

While I was shaken
What did I know?
All I could see was the static
And not eternity
But now I stand as I have waited
And I accept my complete portion
My healing
I am cleansed

The Flame

After the spark
Hence gathers the flame
Of a portion's potential of our soul's need
To sing is to know the possibility
And to find a voice is to recognize again
Nothing escapes the persistence of truth

Flickering
But not afraid
For when you are ready you'll see
How these corners of light stream from an endless source
And how magnified is His desire flowing through empty space
Blues come to an end, fire to burn then project
What was fuel and the end of the age of contempt
Darkness never abides to have access
For to hope is to project all He provides

At Sea

Songs become silence
Once upon no wind,
No sail open to a dream
Anchor's away
I am sent drifting

This becomes the point
Where I look out to find the direction, the discipline
Son, give me something, so as to shine on
There is light, as much as You give me
Give it to me
Then I will rest secure, safe
That You are knowing

This long voyage has me wondering
Was I as ever as lost as time's reassurance?
For in You I will find my destination,
Enlightened
Along a journey in Your rapt attention

Be Whole

Sick of playing not-to-lose
And ending up singing the same refrain
Hallelujah, this day is done?
Some people cannot dream of starving
To be where you are
Don't forsake what it cost
Don't blame yourself at all
While there's mourning for what you cannot explain
And there are more than a million reasons
You're still here
He's not through with you
Everything that is hoped for
Everything of lasting consequence,
Joy and true love
Is bound in this His present
Live and let it come to pass
Breathe and His yoke is easy
There then be whole

That's Right

Walking over a mine of gold
Staring at a sky disguising a shower of diamonds
Bring your shovel/pick/axe
Just try, hold out your hands
Behold an expectation that cannot be defied

The laborer scoffs at the sweat of emancipation
You are rich, as the sun always shines on your portion
A field laden, stars crest-fallen
You cannot keep everything,
It's not yours to redeem
In of yourself,

Petty word---Inheritance, it doesn't come close
To the riches, unfathomed
Stretching spanning eternity
You are clueless
Don't even try
Love so boundless
That's right

Taw

When at last you have spoken
Drawn it out, made it clear
And this is what is left,
What could words say of You?
But even, awe, respect and reverence come short
They fail to describe
What's been in our hearts our whole lives
You are God Almighty
The Eternal Voice of truth
And this is what became in part the praise I could give to You
It is now complete, a declaration:
There is no need to speak any further

LaVergne, TN USA
22 April 2010
180166LV00005B/13/P